A New Tune A Day

for Alto Saxophone

Book 2

Published by
Boston Music Company

Exclusive Distributors:
Music Sales Corporation
257 Park Avenue South, New York, NY 10010, USA.
Music Sales Limited
14-15 Berners Street, London W1T 3LJ, UK.
Music Sales Pty Limited
120 Rothschild Avenue, Rosebery, NSW 2018, Australia.

This book © Copyright 2007 Boston Music Company,
a division of Music Sales Limited

Edited by David Harrison
Music processed by Paul Ewers Music Design
Original compositions and arrangements by Ned Bennett
Cover and book designed by Chloë Alexander
Photography by Matthew Ward
Models: Matthew Deacon and Fran Roper
Printed in the United States of America
Backing tracks by Guy Dagul
CD performance by Ned Bennett
CD recorded, mixed and mastered by Jonas Persson and John Rose

Your Guarantee of Quality
As publishers, we strive to produce every book to the highest commercial
standards. The music has been freshly engraved and the book has been
carefully designed to minimize awkward page turns and to make playing
from it a real pleasure. Throughout, the printing and binding have been
planned to ensure a sturdy, attractive publication which should give years
of enjoyment. If your copy fails to meet our high standards, please inform
us and we will gladly replace it.

www.musicsales.com

This book is not available for sale
outside North and South America.

Boston Music Company
part of The Music Sales Group
London/New York/Paris/Sydney/Copenhagen/Berlin/Madrid/Tokyo

Lesson 21 goals:

1. **The note low C#**
2. **Sixteenth notes**

The note low C#

Exercise 1:

Long low notes are essential for improving your tone.

Breathe in over three seconds and play each note for between five and ten seconds.

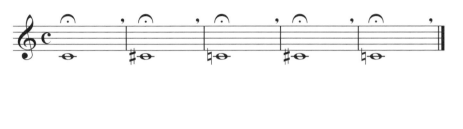

Sixteenth notes

You should already be familiar with notes that last four beats (whole note), two beats (half note), one beat (quarter note), and half a beat (eighth note).

Sixteenth notes last for a *quarter* of the length of a quarter note, or *half* the length of an eighth note.

Single sixteenth note and a sixteenth-note rest

Group of four sixteenth notes (worth one quarter note)

One bar of sixteenth notes in 4/4 time

Exercise 2: Double Or Nothing!

Keep the beat steady and don't start too quickly.

Count: 1234   1 2 3 4   1 2 3 4   1 2 3 4   1   2   3   4   1234

Exercise 3: Three beats per bar

Pieces for Lesson 21

Ballad

Ned Bennett

A ballad is a slow jazz piece. Don't *swing* the eighth notes.

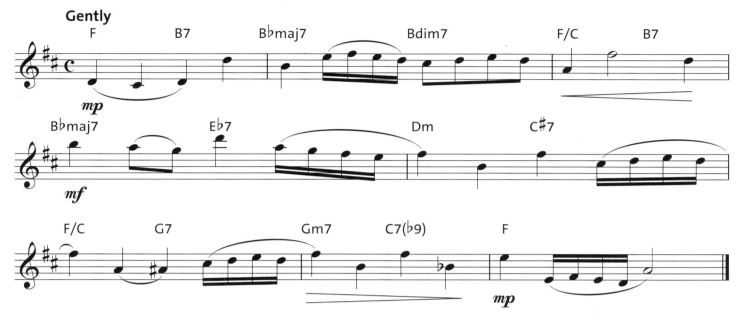

Surprise Symphony (excerpt)

Haydn

The surprise is in the 8th bar of this famous piece. Legend has it that the composer knew that his employer,
Count Esterházy, often fell asleep during concerts. The sudden loud note was to wake him up!

Pieces for Lesson 21

Dracula's Dance

Ned Bennett

Sixteenth notes can look scary at first. Practice this very slowly making sure that your half notes, quarter notes, eighth notes, and sixteenth notes are played in tempo.

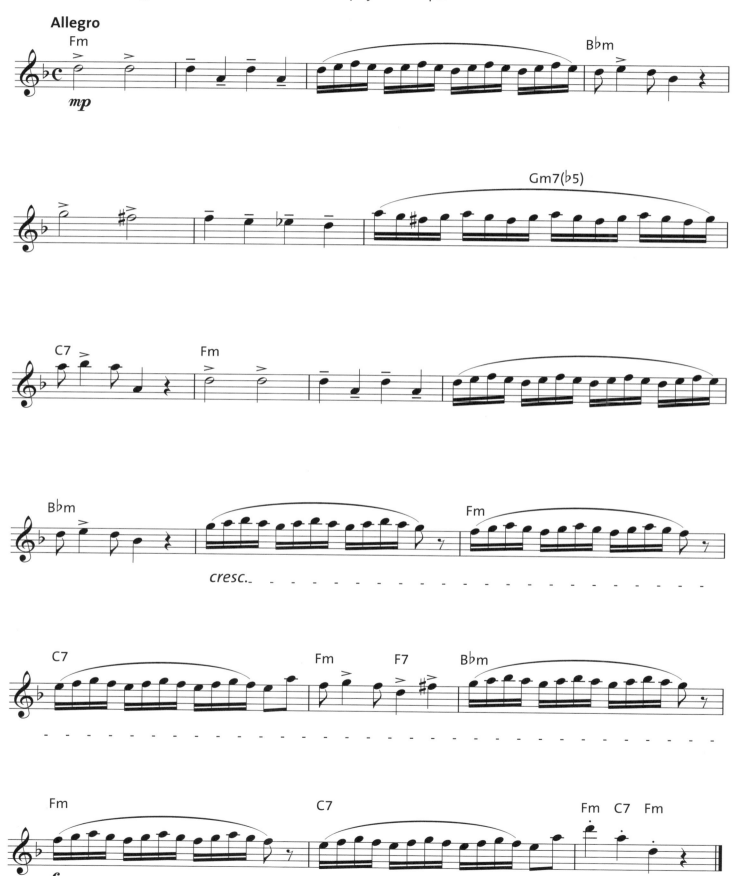

1. **The notes low B and low B flat (B♭)**
2. **Sixteenth-note groups**

The note low B

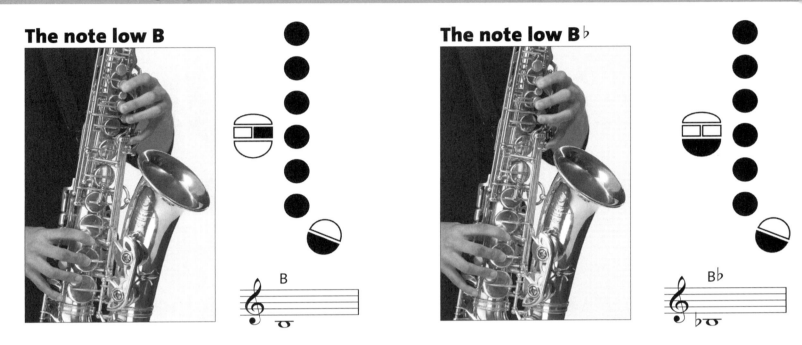

The note low B♭

B♭

Exercise 1:

You will be practicing strength and positions of your little finger, and low notes which require an open throat.

Try to control the volume in this exercise otherwise the neighbors may complain!

In the exercises and pieces of the previous lesson, all the sixteenth notes were in groups of four lasting one beat in total. Below are three commonly seen combinations of eighth notes and sixteenth notes, all grouped together to make up one beat's worth of notes.

Try to learn these patterns as rhythmic words rather than trying to count them each time.

Exercise 2:

Exercise 3:

Exercise 4:

Pieces for Lesson 22

7

Simple Gifts

Joseph Bracket, Jr.

8–9

Frith Street Rag

Ned Bennett

Remember to read the grouped notes as *rhythmic words.*

Moderately

Pieces for Lesson 22

Dance Of The Swans

Tchaikovsky

10–11

TEMPO TERMS

There are a number of articulation markings in this piece including staccato, tenuto, and accent markings.

They occur early in the piece, but you must apply the same articulation later on, even if none is marked, in order to achieve a consistent performance.

Allegretto means "a little *Allegro*," being somewhere between **Andante** and **Allegro** in tempo.

Allegretto

Dotted pairs

The "dotted pair" is a very common rhythm: a dotted eighth note (worth three sixteenth notes) followed by a sixteenth note. Look at these three examples:

The first note of each pair is three times longer than the second. In the final example, the dotted eighth note is worth 3 sixteenth notes. The final sixteenth note completes the group (worth one quarter note in total).

Exercise 1:

It is very important to keep the 3:1 ratio between the dotted pairs, otherwise they could sound like swing eighth notes which are played in a more relaxed way (more like 2:1).

Exercise 2:

Try playing this entire exercise in tempo. Professional musicians often practice scales in this rhythm as it helps develop coordination between the tongue and the fingers.

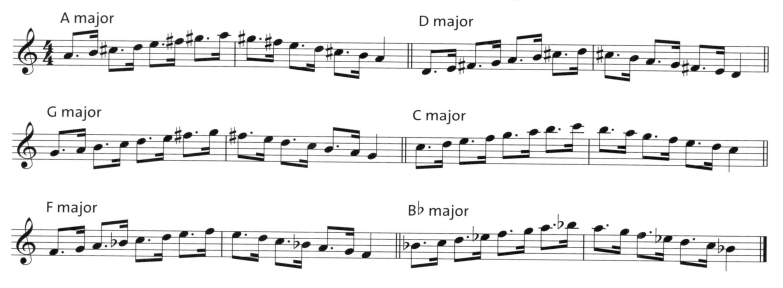

The Scotch snap

The Scotch snap is the opposite of the dotted pair.

The sixteenth note comes first, then the dotted eighth note:

Exercise 3:

Here is a note pattern based on the F major scale using dotted pairs and Scotch snaps. Listen to how this sounds, then try to repeat this exercise in the keys of G, D, and C major.

Pieces for Lesson 23

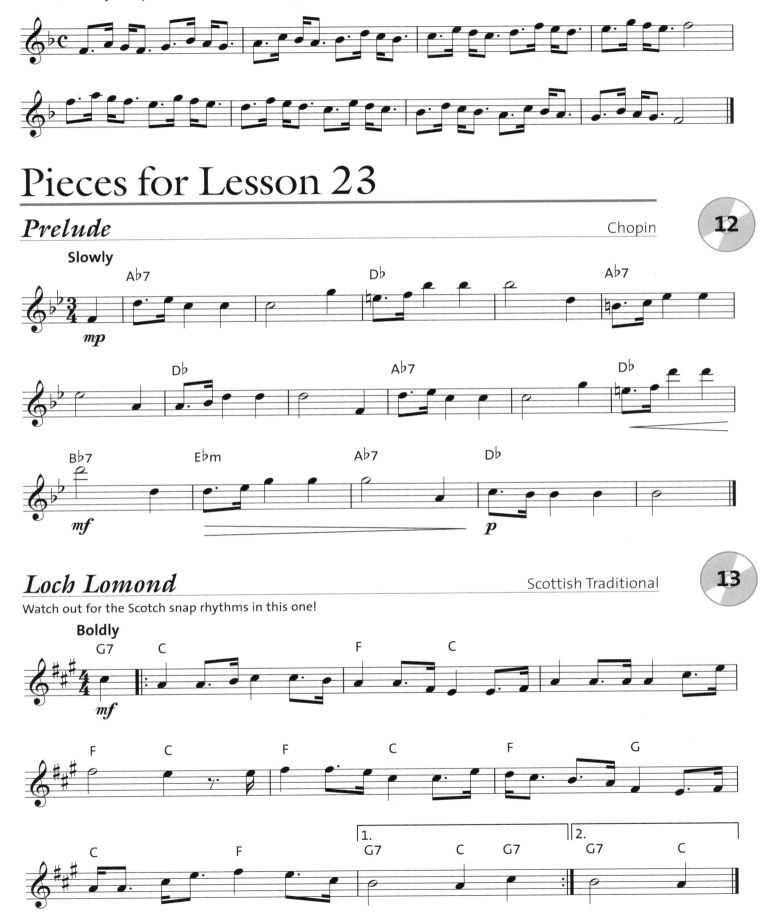

Prelude

Chopin

Loch Lomond

Scottish Traditional

Watch out for the Scotch snap rhythms in this one!

Pieces for Lesson 23

Humoresque

Dvořák

The dotted pairs here are grouped to show each half bar or half note's-worth.

Make sure you don't swing this piece. Keep the dotted pairs light and accurate.

Moderato

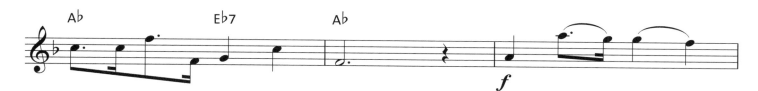

goals:

1. **Playing in tune**
2. **Sixteenth notes in 6/8**

Playing in tune

Expert musicians, no matter what instrument they play, are ones who are fussy about the details relating to their instrument. Here, you are going to focus on one vital detail of saxophone playing.

No saxophone, however expensive, will automatically play in tune. Professional saxophonists make very small adjustments to their embouchure to lower or raise notes by minuscule amounts. These adjustments must become second nature, otherwise there is too much to think about when you are playing a piece.

Exercise 1:

Make sure you have *warmed up* your saxophone.

Play a long F♯ with your correct embouchure (this will be the note A on the piano). Make sure you are perfectly in tune with the piano or CD tuning note. If you are sharp (too high), twist your mouthpiece out a little.

Do the opposite if you are flat (too low).
Your teacher will be able to guide you.

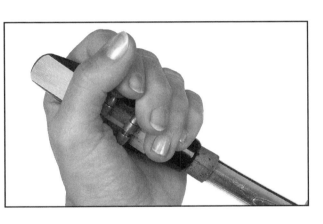

Now play the following music (in tempo) along with the CD or piano, listening very carefully to every note.

If you are in tune, the note will sound pure. If you are sharp, there will be an uncomfortable, grating sound. You will find that you may have to lower the higher notes by dropping your lower jaw a fraction. In this case, apply a little more pressure from your diaphragm to ensure a solid tone.

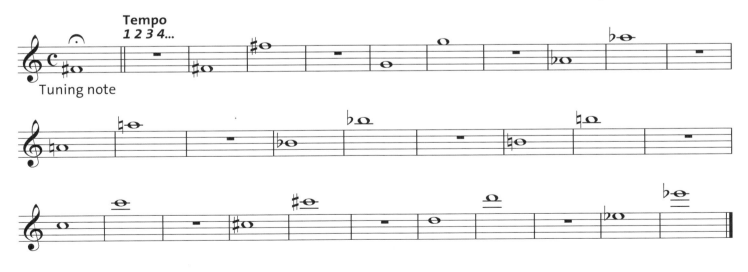

Intonation is the word for tuning individual notes. Good intonation takes a while to achieve.
Play this exercise at least three times a week.

Sixteenth notes in 6/8 time

Below are pairs of sixteenth notes within half a 6/8 bar. As you did with the simple time groups, try to learn these rhythms as words. They have been labeled A to J.

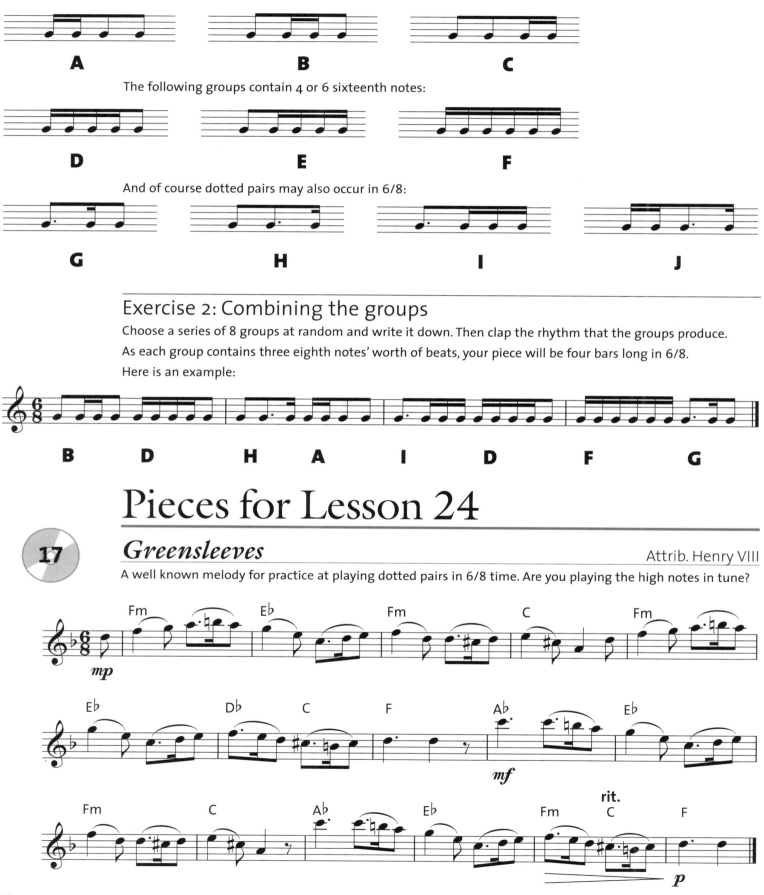

A   B   C

The following groups contain 4 or 6 sixteenth notes:

D   E   F

And of course dotted pairs may also occur in 6/8:

G   H   I   J

Exercise 2: Combining the groups

Choose a series of 8 groups at random and write it down. Then clap the rhythm that the groups produce.

As each group contains three eighth notes' worth of beats, your piece will be four bars long in 6/8.

Here is an example:

B   D   H   A   I   D   F   G

Pieces for Lesson 24

17 *Greensleeves*
Attrib. Henry VIII

A well known melody for practice at playing dotted pairs in 6/8 time. Are you playing the high notes in tune?

Pieces for Lesson 24

Lillabullero

Allegro Moderato

Justano Bardi

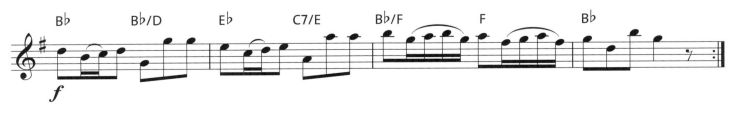

Lesson 25 goals:

1. The chromatic scale
2. Good intonation through duet playing

The chromatic scale

Chromatic literally means "colored." The chromatic scale is colored by every note that can be played on your instrument. Each note is one semitone above or below the last one.

Exercise 1:

Play one octave of the chromatic scale starting on G, ascending and descending.
You will find it is best to use the side B♭ fingering when needed.

Exercise 2:

Now play the chromatic scale starting on E.

Did you notice that this uses exactly the same notes?
You can start and finish the chromatic scale wherever you like, but the notes will always be the same.

Exercise 3:

A chromatic exercise to improve your high notes. Play the repeated bars many times over, slowly at first.
Keep your hand movements to a minimum. Don't forget to check your intonation.

Exercise 4:

Another chromatic exercise to help improve your low notes. You will need strong little fingers for this and lots of patience. This one is Hard (with a capital H)!

Pieces for Lesson 25

When And Where

Ned Bennett

You should learn both parts. Good intonation is vital to make this piece work.

Watch out for chromatic passages.

Slowly

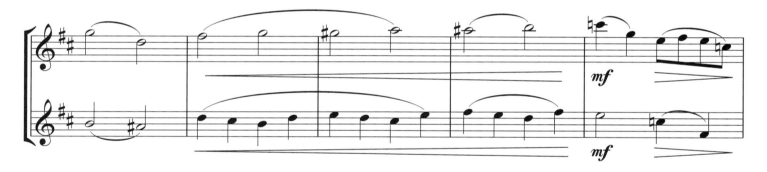

Pieces for Lesson 25

Spring Song

Mendelssohn

Entry Of The Gladiators

Fučík

First practice this famous tune slowly to work out the notes. Don't lose patience...it's well worth the effort!

goals:

1. **The Blues scale**
2. **Improvisation**

The Blues scale

The Blues is a style of music that originated in the American South during the beginning of the 20th century.

Originally a Blues musician would sing while accompanying himself on guitar but, from the 1920s, the Blues was played on piano, saxophone, trumpet, and most jazz instruments.

Most of the melodic content of the Blues uses the Blues scale, a series of notes that gives the music its special character.

Huddie Ledbetter (Leadbelly)

Exercise 1:

There is a Blues scale for every key. Here is the Blues scale in G.

Exercise 2:

Here is a short melody to illustrate how the notes of the Blues scale can sound.
Notice that you can extend the scale above and below the key notes.

Improvisation

One very essential part of Blues (and jazz) is *improvisation*. This means that the musician makes up the melody as he or she goes along. The Blues scale makes this quite easy, as it will fit with all the different chords that accompany the Blues.

Exercise 3:

Make sure you have practiced the G Blues scale so that you can play it without looking.
Play the following four bars. Can't see any notes? Then you'll have to make something up as you go along, but keep the tempo steady!

Pieces for Lesson 26

26-27

Holy-Moly Blues

Ned Bennett

Play the notated bars as written. Improvise the blank bars using only the notes of the G Blues scale. The slashes indicate the beats in these improvised bars. If you can't think of anything to play, either repeat the notated bar you have just played, or don't play at all...rests are a very important part of all music!

28-29

Play This Funky Music

Ned Bennett

Funk is a more modern style than Blues, although it shares many characteristics. Don't swing the eighth notes, and remember to take the *D.C. al Fine* after your improvisation. Sixteen bars may seem like a long time, but it will be over before you know it.

Exercise 4:

Here is the Blues scale in E, ascending and descending over two octaves.

Make sure you can play it fluently and from memory before attempting the next piece.

Alabama Boogie-Woogie

Ned Bennett

30

Traditional Blues uses a 12-bar chord sequence to tie the music together.

This piece follows the 12-bar Blues form. Play the "head" (melody), then two choruses of improvisation, then the head once more, remembering to go to the Coda to finish.

Boogie-Woogie was originally a style of Blues played on the piano. The left hand would play a repeated rhythm throughout that gave the music its driving nature.

Medium Swing Tempo

19

goals:

1. Eighth-note triplets
2. Minor scales

Eighth-note triplets

Triplets are a set of three notes that occupy the time that would normally be taken up by two notes of the same value. Look at the following comparison.

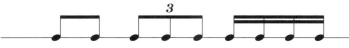

Each of the three groups contains notes that add up to one quarter note. Eighth-note triplets (a group of three eighth notes with a "3" written above or below) must be played faster than ordinary eighth notes, but not as fast at sixteenth notes.

Exercise 1:

Play this with a slow and steady beat. Putting a slight accent on the notes that coincide with a beat.

Count: 1 2 3 4   1 2 3 4   1 2 3 4   1 2 3 4   1...

Exercise 2: Eighth notes and eighth-note triplets

It is easy to make the mistake of playing triplets as a group of two sixteenth notes followed by an eighth note. Make sure all three notes are exactly the same length. Try this tongued and slurred as indicated.

As outlined in book 1, scale practice will help you to:

- Train your fingers to respond quickly in various keys
- Ensure evenness in the timing of notes
- Develop a consistent tone over the range of the instrument
- Increase control over your breathing
- Improve your listening awareness of note relationships

Exercise 3: Two new minor scales:

G minor

E minor

Pieces for Lesson 27

La donna è mobile from Rigoletto

Verdi

31

Here's a very happy tune from a very sad opera. Make sure the dotted pairs are exact.

Barry O'Flynn

Irish Folk Song

32-33

The instruction "with a swing" actually makes this piece easier. Like jazz, many Irish tunes are written down in the way that's easiest to read.

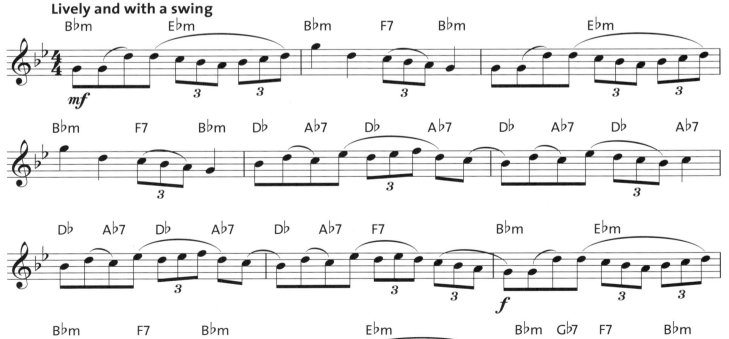

Pieces for Lesson 27

34–35

Valse No. 9 (Op. 69, No. 1)

Chopin

Chopin wrote many extremely fast pieces for piano. However, some of his most beautiful music is slow and lyrical. This must be played exactly as written. Although it looks hard, there is a lot of repetition, and remember: *lento* means "slowly," which will help.

Lento

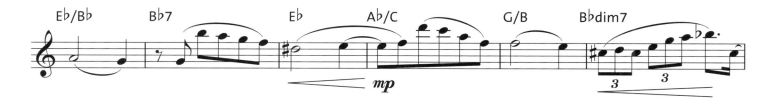

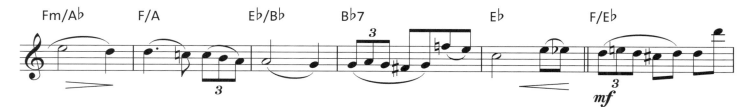

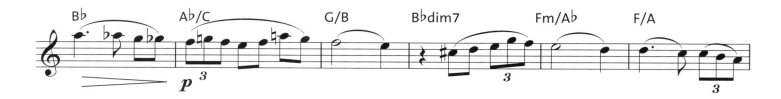

goals:

1. Quarter-note triplets
2. Acciaccaturas

Quarter-note triplets

Just as eighth-note triplets occupy the space of two regular eighth notes, a quarter-note triplet fits into the space of two ordinary quarter notes.

Count: 1   2   3   4   1   2   3   4

You can see the difficulty here is that while the first note of each group of triplets falls on a beat, the second and third fall on either side of the next beat.

Exercise 1:

Play both of the following. What do you notice?

Exercise 2:

The accents are there to help you because they always coincide with beats 1 and 3.
Be careful not to play quarter-note triplets as an eighth note-quarter note-eighth note rhythm.

Acciaccatura

This is a very long word for an extremely short note. An acciaccatura (pronounced atch-akka-tour-a) may be written as a small eighth note or a sixteenth note with a slash through the tail, but should last no time at all and be slurred to the main note. Whether the acciaccatura comes *just before* the beat or right on it is a topic of hot debate in classical circles: let your sense of style and phrasing be your guide!

Exercise 3:

Pieces for Lesson 28

36–37

Triplet Trouble Blues

Ned Bennett

Take this slowly, but still play the acciaccaturas quickly and on the beat, not before.

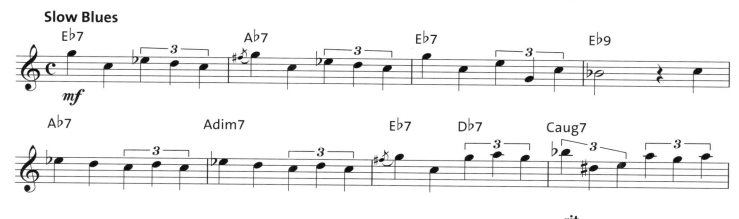

38

To The Spring

Edvard Grieg

Listen to the quarter note count-in very carefully. The accompaniment consists of quarter-note triplets, which may make it difficult for you to find the pulse!

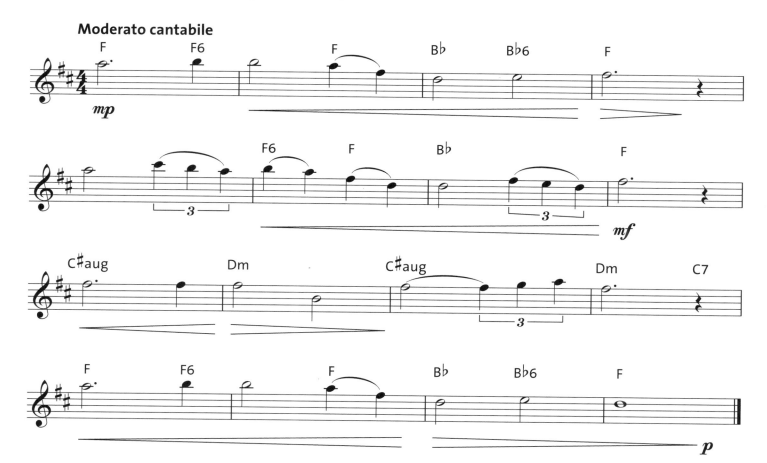

Pieces for Lesson 28

Moment Musical

Schubert

No triplets to worry about here. However, there are plenty of acciaccaturas.

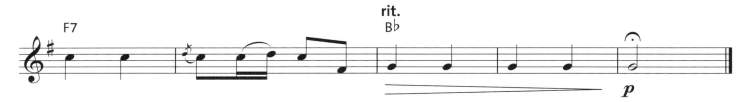

goals:

1. Improving your tone
2. Breath control
3. More dynamics

Improving your tone

There must have been something about the saxophone that made you want to learn to play one. Although the instrument *looks* cool, it has a unique sound that can make the hair on the back of your neck stand on end.

Your tone should be clear, with very little breath noise or hiss. Push enough air through the saxophone to achieve a moderately loud and bright tone that doesn't "wobble." If you are finding this hard, check that your reed is correctly positioned and undamaged.

Try to record yourself playing one of your favorite pieces from this book. You don't have to hire a recording studio: most computers can record sound, and schools and colleges often have a good recording device. Listen to the recording. How do you sound compared to your teacher or your favorite sax player on CD?

A great tone takes years to develop. It is not just knowing what to do, it is also building up muscles (or *chops* as jazz musicians say), just like an athlete would to compete at the highest level.

The following *chops* exercises could be thought of as your saxophone gym routine.
The more you play these exercises, the better you will sound.
You won't need your brain once you are familiar with the exercises, so walk about, or look out the window while playing them.

Try to spend five to ten minutes, three times a week, on this routine.

Chops exercise 1:

Breathe in slowly and deeply.
Play the first note for a count of 4. Slur to the lower note and hold it on for the rest of your breath.
Keep pushing out air, until you really have none left in your lungs.
Relax, breathe in slowly and play the next pair. (In the 2nd pair, play the G♯ as a G with the low C♯ key held down.)

This exercise is to:

- Build muscles so you can keep your throat open at all times when playing
- Enlarge your lung capacity and control your airflow using your diaphragm
- Build muscles in both little fingers

Chops exercise 2:

Breathe as you did for Chops exercise 1, but only one note per breath here. Do not change the fingering for any of the notes. The first note is played with an open throat. To get the second note, increase the speed of the air by pushing a little more with your diaphragm and tighten your bottom lip slightly without closing your jaw. The third note requires an even firmer bottom lip.

Try not to tighten your embouchure to get these higher notes otherwise the tone will be thin. If you can, concentrate on moving your jaws slightly further apart by dropping your chin.

Practice this in front of a mirror. Check that your embouchure appears "round" and not "wide."

This exercise is to:

- Build muscles so you can keep your throat open at all times when playing
- Improve your diaphragm control
- Enlarge your mouth cavity to produce a fuller and sweeter tone
- Build muscle strength in your bottom lip

Remember—keep the fingering for low C throughout.

Dynamic Extremes

Up till now you have played music with dynamics ranging anywhere from quiet to loud (*p* to *f*).
As your strength and control increases, you could be asked to play very quiet (*pianissimo*) *pp*, or very loud (*fortissimo*) *ff*.

Chops exercise 3:

Breathe in slowly and deeply. Play each note for as long as possible, moving very slowly and perfectly smoothly through the dynamics as indicated. Ensure that all notes are in tune.

This exercise is to:

- Increase your diaphragm control
- Improve your intonation
- Improve your tone by building muscles through long notes

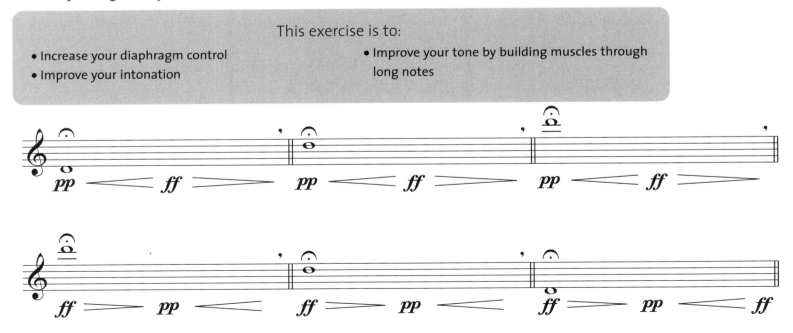

Pieces for Lesson 29

41

Adagietto from Symphony No. 5

Mahler

This should be slow, and very expressive—it ranks among the most passionate music ever written.

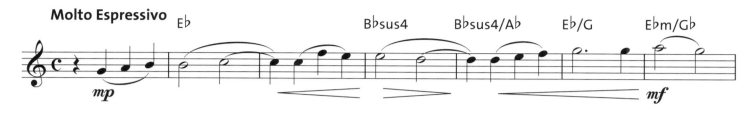

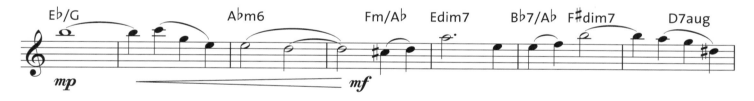

goals:

1. Practice routine
2. Trills

Practice routine

There is one basic fact that applies to playing every musical instrument: **the more you practice, the quicker you will improve**. Some people enjoy practicing and others don't. However, a fixed daily routine is essential to make the best of your time.

- Try to practice at the same time every day
- Be focused: keep your mind entirely on your practicing
- Remember your goals for the week (new pieces, scales, etc.)

- Spend a good amount of time on technical work; don't just play your favorite pieces
- Don't be impatient: remember that you will be a better player for having practiced

Use the following table to log your practice for this week.
Be honest...this is to help you work out how to improve at a quicker pace.

Day	Long note warm-ups	Chops *or* Intonation Exercise		Scales	Pieces	Total minutes
		Chops	**Intonation**			

Trills

Although usually found in music from the Baroque era (1600-1750) and the Classical era (1750-1820), trills are a very important form of ornamentation in many styles of music. The written note is rapidly alternated with the note above:

Not exact sixteenth notes, just as fast as possible.

For music written before 1750, begin the trill on the upper note.

Pieces for Lesson 30

Gavotte from Suite No. 3

J. S. Bach (1685-1750)

Look at Bach's dates: on which notes do the trills begin?

* Use the side B♭ fingering here. Keep the side key pressed as you alternate with the C.

Pieces for Lesson 30

Flor, Bianca Flor

Mexican Folk Song

This is from the 19th century. Keep the rhythm straight, although there is room for expressive playing.

Your trills should be coordinated if possible.

goals:

1. Rubato
2. Solo playing

Rubato

Sometimes, subtly altering the tempo during a piece of music can be very expressive.
Soloists often use a kind of hesitation, or slowing down, to achieve a dramatic effect.
This is known as *rubato* (Italian for "robbed") and is especially effective when used sparingly.

Originally rubato passages "borrowed" time by slowing down, and then caught up with the accompaniment by speeding up later in the phrase. Nowadays playing rubato simply means being flexible with the tempo of the performance to create expression.

A good soloist will know the music by heart. This gives the performer confidence and helps the music to flow much more convincingly.

Solo playing

In most music auditions, an unaccompanied piece tests your ability to play *solo*. You may also be asked to perform in a concert, or you may want to play for your friends and family.

A guide for solo playing

• If the piece has a lively rhythm, it is essential that you keep the beat steady. Music is a language, and if people can tap their toes to what you are playing, you are communicating with them.

• Never perform a piece so fast that you have to slow down for the tricky passages. Practice everything at one tempo and gradually speed up the whole piece.

• If the piece is dreamier in nature, then allow yourself some rubato. Enjoy the feeling of power that you can control your audience. Make them wait for expressive moments, or increase their excitement by pushing the tempo a little faster.

• Whatever the piece, always think before you play. Try to hear the beginning of the piece in your head... breathe...breathe again... then play.

Solo Pieces for Lesson 31

Sailor's Hornpipe

English Folk Dance

Traditionally this piece begins very slowly and gradually builds up tempo to a fast, rousing conclusion.
However, make sure you can play it all perfectly at a moderate tempo before you try anything fancy.

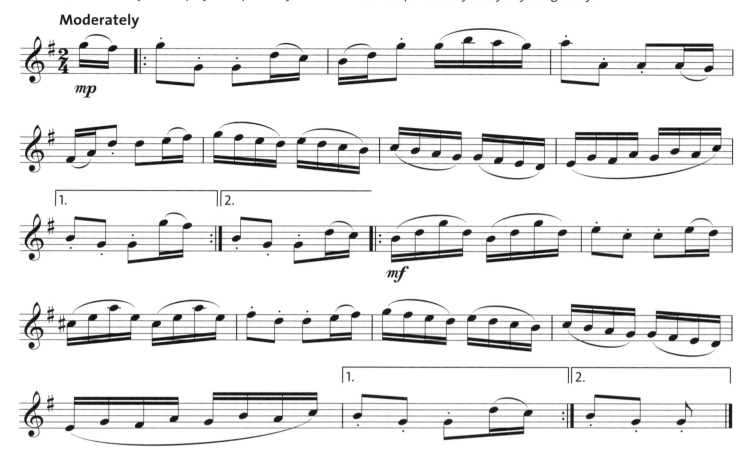

Sometimes I Feel Like A Motherless Child

Spiritual

Here's an opportunity for rubato. Learn the piece keeping to a strict, slow tempo. Then think how you might
make it more expressive by changing this at times.

100% Humidity

Ned Bennett

Swing this piece which uses the E Blues scale. Keep the tempo steady (no rubato), and repeat the improvisation section as many times as you like. You must always relate the notes to the beat which should remain implied by what you play. Take the ideas for your improvisation from the written music if you wish.

Medium Shuffle

goals:

1. **Simple time, compound time, and unusual time signatures**
2. **More scales**

Time signatures

In *simple* time signatures the beat can be divided into two. It means that the music flows predictably and this is why these signatures are the most commonly found:

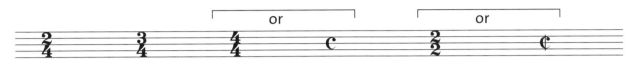

In *compound* time signatures the beat divides into three. The music still flows well.

| one beat | two beats | three beats | four beats |

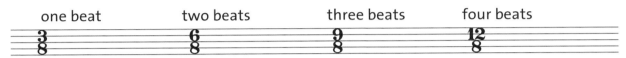

All the pieces that you have played so far in this book use a time signature from the illustrations above. However, many pieces deliberately use a less-flowing time signature:

Exercise 1:

Clap the following examples, emphasizing the notes on which accents have been placed.

By the way, the time signature may change at any point in a piece! Have a look at the *Bulgarian Dance* later in this lesson to see an example of this.

Lesson 32

Exercise 2: New scales and arpeggios

Scale:

E♭ major

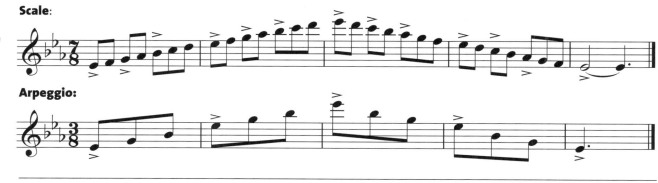

Arpeggio:

Scale:

F# minor

Play these according to the time signatures and accents (although normally you should play them with equal weighting for each note).

Arpeggio:

Pieces for Lesson 32

46–47

Bulgarian Dance

Energetically

Pieces for Lesson 32

Ut tuo propitiatus

11th Century Organum

At first this piece may sound odd, perhaps rather modern and experimental, even though it was written almost a thousand years ago.

Try to find a church or large hall with lots of reverberation in which to play it. Originally this would have been sung by monks. However, the sound of two saxophones can be equally as haunting.

Don't play this fast, and stick to a strict tempo until the very end.

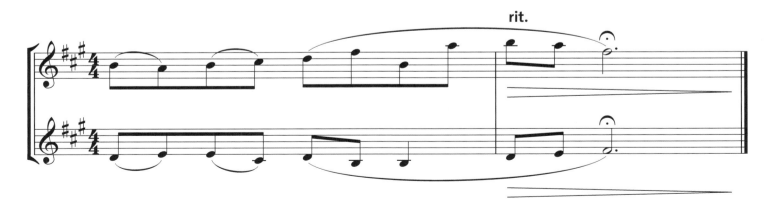

Lesson 33 goals:

1. Dexterity
2. Increasing speed

Dexterity

You may have listened to a piece of music that is so fast you can hardly hear the individual notes. When played well, this can sound impressive and exciting. However, it takes a long time and endless patience to develop the skill needed to play very quickly.

Exercise 1:

Practice these exercises regularly, instead of (or in addition to) your intonation and chops exercises.

This exercise uses patterns of the first three notes of every major scale. Make sure you spend more time with the patterns you can't play very well in order to play the whole exercise at a reasonable tempo, both slurred and tongued (which is hard!).

The first key has been written out in full. Play the rest in the same manner.

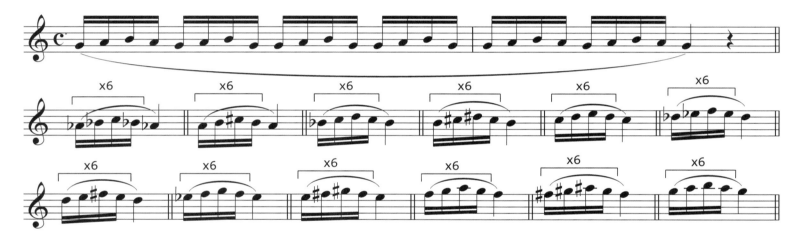

Exercise 2:

This one is chromatic and happens to work down through the keys, but you could equally work up.

Your little fingers (and side keys) will get a real workout here.

38

Pieces for Lesson 33

Caprice No. 24 (theme)

Paganini

Presto means fast. This piece was originally written for violin, but it has been arranged for piano, cello, and jazz band as well as saxophone.

The Irish Washer Woman

Irish 18th Century

Coordination between your tongue and fingers is essential for this piece.

Czardas

Monti

Play the first (slow) section with just a little rubato. The second section needs to be very fast.

As with all fast music, practice it slowly but in tempo otherwise you will never learn the correct timing.

goals:

1. Endurance
2. Sensitivity

Playing for any length of time puts a strain on your embouchure muscles. Think of running an 800 meter race. The first lap is usually okay, but you will feel the pain in your legs during the second lap. This is because when you tighten your muscles, blood cannot flow through them. Your embouchure muscles go through the same process in a long piece.

To avoid this pain, ensure you release all tension in your bottom lip every time you breathe. Even relaxing for a fraction of a second can allow the blood to flow with its precious oxygen.

Don't forget to be sensitive to the other musicians. In this piece you will sometimes have an interesting melody, but sometimes you will be accompanying other players. Adjust your dynamic level (volume) to reflect this during this 16th century masterpiece.

Alla riva del Tebro (madrigal)
Palestrina

Although the notes in this quartet seem easy, playing it will be hard. Keep your bottom lip relaxed, and make sure you count like crazy. If you get lost you will find it almost impossible to find your place again.

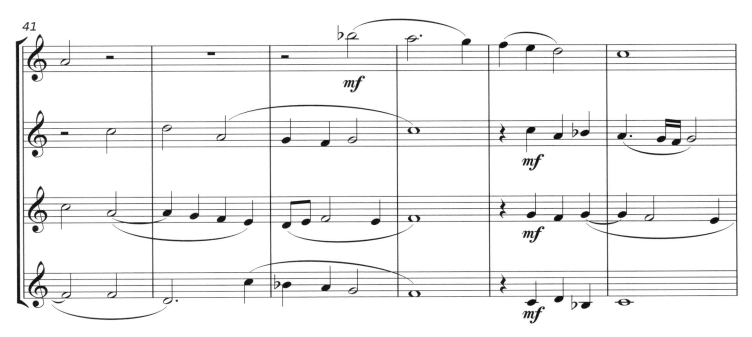

1. Concert Performance

Concert Performance

Having worked through books 1 and 2 of *A New Tune A Day*, you should be ready to perform as part of a concert, whether for friends and family, at school, or for an audience you've never met.

Give yourself the best chance of success with these golden rules.

1. Know your music.
You must be able to play all your pieces, perfectly and without thinking. Musicians play much better if they have memorized the music.

2. Look the part.
Dress professionally, and present yourself as you would for meeting someone very important. This will help you to feel confident when you play.

3. Breathe slowly and deeply before you play.
This will help overcome nerves and oxygenate your brain, helping you to concentrate. It also lets you pause to think about the piece.

4. Bow slowly to the audience when they clap.
This is good manners, as if to say "thank you for listening to me."

Pieces for Lesson 35

The following pieces are all great for a performance. Even if you are playing them just for practice or fun, imagine you are giving a live performance and play with all the expression, technique, and accuracy you can.

 52·53

Wedding Dance

Kazakhstan

Here is a fiddly melody with many complications, but rewarding to play if you practice it carefully.

Energetic

F and C ped. accomp.

Pieces for Lesson 35

Waltz from Die Fledermaus

Strauss

This is a fine, flowing waltz that needs lots of energy to perform.

This piece is always performed as part of the New Year's Day concert in Vienna, Austria.

Pieces for Lesson 35

56–57

Oh, Won't You Sit Down

Spiritual

This piece has been arranged in a jazz style. Play swing eighth notes, and instead of the written notes, play a
G Blues scale improvisation in the section marked *solo ad lib* if you prefer.

Pieces for Lesson 35

Hungarian Dance No. 5

Brahms

58·59

Finally, an exciting romp to finish the book. Watch out for the tempo changes towards the end, and make sure your fingers know the notes by themselves.

CD track listing

How to use the CD

The tuning note on track 1 is concert A, which sounds the same as F♯ on the alto saxophone. Look for the symbol in the book for the relevant backing track.

123456789